CHAMPIONS
IN THE
MAKING

BOOK TWO: Motivating Kids

J. ZINK, Ph.D.

OTHER PUBLICATIONS ON CHILD DEVELOPMENT

BY DR. ZINK:

CHAMPIONS IN THE MAKING
BOOK ONE: *Building Positive Self-Concept in Kids* (J. ZINK, INC., 1981)
(formerly titled BREAKFAST FOR CHAMPIONS: BUILDING
POSITIVE SELF-CONCEPT IN KIDS).

CHAMPIONS IN THE MAKING
BOOK THREE: *Ego States* (J. ZINK, INC., 1986)

CHAMPIONS ON THE SCHOOL BUS: A SCHOOL BUS DRIVER'S
GUIDE TO POSITIVE DISCIPLINE ON THE SCHOOL BUS (J. ZINK,
INC., 1982).

CHAMPIONS IN THE LIBRARY: A LIBRARIAN'S GUIDE TO
POSITIVE DISCIPLINE IN THE LIBRARY (J. ZINK, INC., 1982).

CHAMPIONS IN THE MAKING: A POSITIVE APPROACH TO
DISCIPLINE (AUDIO TAPE) J. ZINK, INC., 1982.

A POSITIVE APPROACH TO DISCIPLINE (VIDEO TAPE) J. ZINK,
INC., 1982.

THE COMPLETE CHAMPIONS WORKSHOP (AUDIO TAPES) J.
ZINK, INC., 1986.

"I regard human motivation as very eccentric and peculiar."

Dr. John McCarthy
"The Dean of Artificial Intelligence"
Psychology Today
January, 1983

"Motivation is born of a will to succeed. Nothing builds a positive self-concept in a kid like the sense of success."

Dr. J. Zink
Keynote address
State Education Association
Omaha, Nebraska
October, 1982

I wish to acknowledge here the love, support, and contributions of my wife of sixteen years, Kern Walsh, and our son, Joe. You two for me are the force that through the green fuse drives the flower.

Dr. J. Zink
Manhattan Beach,
California
1983

ISBN 0-942490-02-9

FIRST PRINTING, AUGUST, 1983
SECOND PRINTING, OCTOBER, 1984
THIRD PRINTING, APRIL, 1987
FOURTH PRINTING, MAY, 1988

Special thanks to Len and Janet Davis for typing and printing this book.

Printed in U.S.A. by Iwate Printing, 13616 Normandie Ave., Gardena, CA 90247

This Book is For

CECELIA FELDMEIER ZINK,

The Motivator's Motivator

TABLE OF CONTENTS

Part One:

UNDERSTANDING MOTIVATION

And the wine having run short, the mother of Jesus said to him, "They have no wine." And Jesus said to her, "What wouldst thou have me do, woman? My hour has not yet come." His mother said to the attendants, "Do whatever he tells you."

St. John
Chapter 2
Verses 3-5

Chapter One:
INTRODUCTION

Some time ago I finished writing my first book for Parents and Teachers on the subject of positive discipline. It is now titled *CHAMPIONS IN THE MAKING, BOOK ONE: BUILDING POSITIVE SELF-CONCEPT IN KIDS.* When it was first published it was called *BREAKFAST FOR CHAMPIONS.* The book is not about a famous breakfast cereal (which is, in part, why I changed the title) but it did reach out and touch parents and teachers in a special way. From all over the world they wrote to me with wonderful messages of encouragement and love. They **demanded** that I write a second book, or sequel to the first. They said they liked my simple writing style and appreciated that I wrote to help and not impress with fancy words or psychological jargon. One woman told me that I had saved her marriage because she and her husband fought constantly about the kids until they read my book. One man told me that I gave him a discovery of his son as a person and not an object. He said my book showed him how to be friends with his son. He said "May God bless your life forever." Another man came up to me after one of my lectures and told me "I love you for what you are doing for children."

Not long ago I visited the classroom of a second grade teacher who read my book and attended one of my lectures. I noticed that one little boy was parked in the "Penalty Box" at the side of the room. When I asked him why he was there, he said, "I made a bad choice and now I've been Zinked." Recently, 1000 students at Ponchatoula High School in Ponchatoula, Louisiana, invited me to speak to them on the subject of self-discipline. They gave me a beautiful plaque which thanks me for teaching their teachers classroom discipline. And when I finished speaking to them, they stomped their feet and chanted ZINK! ZINK! ZINK! I loved it. These experiences have changed my life in a dramatic way. Each time someone applauds my work, I am motivated to do more, work harder, give more lectures, and **write more books**.

The point is this: even though I understand the forces of human motivation, they are at work on me. They are changing my own behavior in very powerful and significant ways. They drive me to sit at my desk and write these words instead of playing tennis, walking by the ocean, or taking a hike in the deep, dark, and quiet woods. *"But I have promises to keep,"* Robert Frost, himself a driven man, wrote to describe the driving force of motivation.

When a lot of people one considers special get very excited about one's work, then one **cannot** resist the powerful and compelling urge to do more work. It is, at once, the beginning of satisfaction and the dawn of the quest for "self-discovery."

Self-discovery is our goal as parents and teachers for all of our children. When, at last, they have a dream which is a clear vision of what uses they have for their lives, **and** they have the basic skills to make those uses reality, then our job is finished. We stand in awe, then, cheering them on to new victories.

We must realize that as parents and teachers, we are the most important people on the face of the earth for our children. What we think of them, say to them, and do **not** say to them is more important in the shaping of their development than what anyone else **in the world** says to them. Not always are they our world; **always**, (in the beginning years), we are theirs.

I do not believe that the phenomenon of Wolfgang Amadeus Mozart happened as a lone and isolated miracle; that when he struck his first piano key, no one was near to applaud with enthusiasm and shout with glee. Little Wolfgang was born into a musical family and his house was filled with musical instruments and people who could play them well. So when the child, who no doubt had natural inclinations and innate talent, touched the keys to the clavichord for the first time, he was bombarded with oohs and ahhs and wunderbars. How quickly he learned the way to get fantastic and immediate attention! Most kids only get that kind of emotional response when they reach for the stove or heave their cereal.

One of the keys to understanding human motivation lies in the power of the emotional response others give to our behavior. Kids who draw powerful emotional responses for being lazy, causing disruptions, fighting with their brothers and sisters, going through your drawers when you're on the phone, taping shut the cat's eyes, and squirting super glue into your car door locks have learned how to get your complete and total attention. If you give few other behaviors complete and total attention, they have learned that anger, frustration and rage are far superior to no attention at all. Most kids get motivated in a positive direction when they experience success at getting the positive emotional attention of others. At the base of the successful experience, like learning to tie one's shoes, learning to sew an even buttonhole, learning to feel the clutch grab as it comes up and the gas pedal goes down (on a hill, no less, what a wonderful feeling!) is a common denominator for all human beings. From the success of these activities and others like them we learn how to feel good about being ourselves. And learning to feel good about ourselves and our activities lies at the heart of all motivation.

Ever ask yourself why young boys who will not sit still to read a paragraph (the wooden desks are so uncomfortable!) will sit for hours on end (theirs) on cold and unforgiving garage floor cement to tinker with the inner mysteries of a rear wheel bicycle axle? Or spend days or weeks hunched over in prayer to the great video god, Pac-Man? Whether it is lights, bells, and whistles or tiny little gears that fit oh so close together, it **feels so good** when you master it! "Take it to Neil. Neil can fix anything. He is a mechanical wizard," or "That's Tony Roffino. 11 million points on the Tron at the arcade. That's radical." The point to this discussion about learning to feel good about oneself is this: the emotional state of feeling good when one discovers, masters, or overcomes is a psychological fact that parents and teachers **overlook** often when dealing with under motivated kids.

Skillful parents and teachers understand that successful experiences for kids which generate the honest emotional state of feeling good about oneself **can be arranged**. Giving kids the responsibility for certain tasks is one way of arranging the success which preceeds the feeling of accomplishment. This begins what I call "The Motivation Cycle." In order to understand how powerful it is, consider the story of Cathy. Cathy's parents first came to see me after Cathy, age 16, had gone through two abortions.

Her older brother, Carl, age 19, was addicted to cocaine. This habit cost him more than $300 per day and to support it, in part, he was a thief. Cathy's parents are extremely wealthy and could, if they so desired, support Carl's habit forever. But the purpose of their visit to me was to get help for Cathy. They considered Carl, at 19, to be "lost." Cathy had run away from home several times and openly defied and ignored her parents' authority. In the initial interview with Cathy's parents, I learned that they had been married for twenty-four years to each other. And, for the last seven years, they had taken no vacation because they were afraid to leave the house. Cathy and about 100 of her "friends" had nearly destroyed the house once during a "party." When Cathy came to see me, I discovered a thirty-five year old mind in a sixteen year old body. She was very cynical, sometimes bitter, and very blase about her intense familiarity with drugs, alcohol, and sex. But I got her attention quickly when I asked her if she knew how long her parents had been married. She didn't know. And her eyes opened very wide when I told her that twenty-four years was a very great achievement and wasn't it a shame they had not gone on vacation in seven years? When I asked her how she felt about that, she said, "Rotten." So I told her I had an idea. I said "wouldn't it be great if your parents would feel comfortable going on a romantic weekend to San Francisco. You know, two nights at the Sir Francis Drake, candlelight dinners, a little dancing, walks in the moonlight on the wharf. . ." Cathy said her parents would never go. I told her that I had trained her parents in the use of a positive discipline plan for her. I said I taught them how to write rules for her behavior. These included what time she should be home, her use of the telephone, her use of drugs and alcohol, their position on unprotected sexual intercourse, and her school attendance and homework commitment. I told Cathy that her discipline plan included what they would do if she followed the rules and what they would do if she didn't.

And then I set the bait.

I said "But Cathy, I think you could get something more than they are offering."

"What?"

"I think you could bargain with them so that if you followed all the house rules on your discipline plan for a month, they would spend a weekend together in San Francisco."

Here, indeed, was a novel reward for the girl whose parents had given her everything. The plan worked without a hitch. The first principle of motivation says we are most greatly motivated to do things which make us **feel good** about ourselves. Cathy needed to learn how to earn a sense of feeling good about herself. My plan for her was perfect. I told her the toughest part of the novel plan would **not** be following the rules. The toughest part would be convincing her parents that she would behave while they were gone. But, I said, you can do this because you are so strong. And she did. Her father told me that the scariest drive of his life was from the airport to his home after a wonderful weekend with his wife in San Francisco. He said when they pulled into the drive, Cathy was waiting with all the lights on. The house was immaculate.

No cigarette butts in ashtrays; no dirty dishes in the sink. Cathy wore a dress to welcome them home. He said the last time he saw her in a dress was at her First Holy Communion. Not all case studies have such dramatically successful conclusions but the Cathy story is worth considering because it illustrates such a fundamental aspect of motivation.

We feel because we are the adults and the professionals it is our duty and job to **give** to them. We often do not realize how successful they **feel** when we give them the opportunities to give something to us. The drive to give and the need to be needed can and should be engendered in our children if, as adults, they are to feel a deep sense of personal fulfillment. This feeling must be learned. To be learned it must be earned. Teaching kids how to earn the positive emotion of feeling good about themselves for doing things right and doing the right things is what this book is all about.

NOTES

Part Two:

OLD PROBLEMS
AND
NOVEL SOLUTIONS

To what then shall I liken the men of this generation? And what are they like? They are like children sitting in the market place, calling to one another and saying, "We have piped to you and you have not danced; we have sung dirges, and you have not wept."

St. Luke
Chapter 7
Verses 31, 32

Chapter Two:

THE MOTIVATION CYCLE

There are five observable stages to the motivation cycle for kids. I call them the five R's. They are Risk, Recognition, Review, Rededication, and Readjustment. Let's look at them in order.

The first stage is called Risk. It is the most frightening stage and to understand it fully is to gain insight into the terror of procrastination.

All new activities involve greater psychological risk for kids than they do for adults. Generally, adults have developed sophisticated defense mechanisms against the possibility of failure. They say "bad luck," or "story of my life," or with a weak laugh, "I never was very good at numbers anyway," and move on quickly to something they feel comfortable doing.

Seldom are we adults trapped for very long into doing what makes us miserable. If we are, then, in very short order, bad things begin to happen. We drink heavily, file for divorce, change jobs frequently, take valium, take longer and longer business trips, fantasize about crimes and fool-proof escapes, and maybe even go a little and sometimes a lot crazy. We can't stand being trapped into repeated failure because it doesn't make us feel good about ourselves. Kids on the other hand, are often trapped into facing the same failures at school day after day. Let's face it, if you can't figure out the answer to the word problem, and no one figures out why you cannot understand the process of arriving at word problem solutions, then not only do you **never** learn how to cope with word problems, each time you face a word problem your stomach tightens and you become nervous, anxious, and unhappy with yourself. And when your friends see your bad grade on the test, they say "You can't do word problems? They are so easy" and you feel worse. Then your mom, who can't do word problems either, says "You'll have to get your father to help you with those." This she says only if your father lives there. And when your father gets home, he is tired and out of patience which he freely gives to strangers all day. Also, he lacks the skill to break down the steps to solving word problems into understandable, learnable sequences. So your life is lived to avoid word problems. For those of you who know the experience, you will feel your stomach tighten as I write, "two trains left the station traveling at fifty miles an hour in opposite directions but ten minutes apart. . ."

For those of you who love word problems, you are frustrated that I did not finish the sentence because already you were anticipating the recognition stage, or the subject of our next discussion. This is true because your risk stage for this problem hardly **exists**. You have had success at this activity before.

If a child has many areas of his or her life, like athletics, school work, peer relationships, parent relationships, etc., where risk taking has lead to avoidance of the whole situation, you can see how difficult it can be to motivate this child to do much of anything. And the problem gets compounded as this child becomes a teenager, because a teenager is, in most ways, a brand-new adult. Skills that the pre-teenager had may not carry through puberty. Hence the often repeated negative, "I swear, Martin, you had more manners at age three than you do at age fourteen. Bring the soup to your mouth with a spoon. Don't stick your face in the bowl like a dog!"

The second stage of the motivation cycle is called Recognition. Kids reach this stage when they realize the extent of the effort it will take to accomplish the task. Even though many children will accept the risk of possible failure, or underestimate the task to get through the risk stage, they will stop trying when they recognize how far they must go for success. This is why telling a kid she must get a Ph.D. to be truly successful at math will not motivate her to do work in the sixth grade. Success, like all things great and small, is very relative. Telling a sixth grader that success in math is doing all the problems and double checking her answers before she goes to bed is more realistic; but for someone who has **never** done this before, it is over-reach. This is why she cries when you insist that every single problem be complete, double checked, and perfect before she leaves that table! In her recognition stage of the motivation cycle, she agrees with herself to fail. Once she has agreed to failure, the night is lost to math. Kids who see that the size and scope of the challenge exceeds their ability to imagine what it feels like to win at the challenge search for substitute behaviors. They cry. They get angry. They play with the cat or tease their little brothers. They, in desperation, brighten with the memory to write a thank-you note to Aunt Cis for the Barbie Doll clothes, but they are lost to success at math in the second stage of the motivation cycle. If you, as a teacher or parent, can get them **back on task** at this critical second stage you have scored a major victory. Many parents and teachers use force and threats at this stage. They do so because force and threats **seem** to produce results in many kids. ("I gave him a choice: write the paragraph or die. He chose to write.") In fact, force and threats **ruin the successful feeling** one normally gets at completing a task. Since we do what helps us feel good about ourselves, bad feelings about a particular activity produce guaranteed future failure at the recognition stage, which is only the **second** stage, in a five stage process. As one may see, it is easy to understand why our schools produce more failure than success.

My story of a boy I will call Peter Duncan is appropriate here. Peter, age 12, told me he would rather be paddled than be forced to write a paragraph as a consequence for breaking any rules in class. I told him I thought paddling kids was stupid and he looked at me like he was seeing me for the first time. I told him, "Peter in my class we write and I expect you to write **all the time** you are in my class. Now, sit down, pick up your pencil and write."

He was shocked. Because someone had labeled him "Educationally Handicapped," he had gotten the message that he was not expected to work. So, he DID NOT. I told him in my class he would work. After one hour he had written two words on a blank page. A **typical** teacher response to this might be, "Two words in an hour? Can you afford it?"

This kind of blatant sarcasm said to Peter and in front of his friends **will not** motivate him to write more words on the page.

My response to Peter was calculated to take him by surprise. I flexed my knees so I was eye level with him, looked directly into his eyes, and I said, "Peter, I like your style. This is a great start and your greatest output to date. Tomorrow more words!"

These things I said with sincerity and emotional intensity that proved I meant it. The results of my effort were dramatic. The next day Peter wrote three words. Before you laugh, realize that three words after two words is a 50 percent improvement. I continued my enthusiasm for his work, telling him I was proud of the way he was handling the challenge of writing. By the end of the first week of class, he wrote his first complete topic sentence. By the end of the three weeks, Peter had written a model paragraph, complete with topic, developmental, and summatory sentences. After six weeks, he wrote a "term paper" of six consecutive paragraphs with this title, "What It Feels Like To Be Called Retardo." If I live to write a hundred books, I may never achieve what Peter achieved in six paragraphs. The point is this: sarcasm and snide comments will kill motivation in the recognition stage because this is the stage that takes the most commitment and energy. But love and emotional intensity can light fires large enough to burn to the end of the project. Not to mention brighten a life.

Instead, many teachers feel they must downgrade a student's work in order to spur him or her to greater achievements. This will work only for students whose self-concept is positive. A student who lacks self-confidence will **never** be motivated by poor grades. This same logic makes as much sense as the famous "bell curve." Teachers who believe in the bell curve of grade distribution are actually proud when they produce a perfect curve for a hundred students—10 A's, 20 B's, 40

C's, 20 D's and 10 F's. Put another way, many teachers are happiest when their work results in the triumph of mediocrity. This, of course, is not the fault of the teachers. Very few teachers actually understand what does motivate children even though they **work with children every day**! This is because teachers have not received proper training to do their jobs. In education courses they study far more **subject** matter than classroom behavior management or child motivation. Worse, the typical college professor teaching teacher preparation courses is **experientially** unaware that kids have changed so dramatically in the last ten years. This is true because child-rearing practices have changed. In the early 1960's—just twenty years ago— 1 out of every 20 kids lived with a single parent. In 1982, 1 out of 5 lived with a single parent; in some communities in America that figure is 1 out of 2! When the kids come home, **no one is there**. Mother is working. Some kids go to the day care center at six am, to school at eight am, to the day care center at three pm, and home to an exhausted mother at six pm.

So when this child fails at the second stage of the motivation cycle, neither mother nor dad is there to get the child **back on task**. And when this kid goes to school in the morning, without homework completed, the teacher puts his or her name on the board for some good old-fashioned public humiliation, writes a nasty note home to mother who is frustrated to tears, who in turn yells and threatens capital punishment if the word problems are not done before nine o'clock tonight, young lady. Do you understand me and have I made myself clear?

And so it goes.

If you never make it past the second stage—recognition of the scope of the task—you will never succeed. Some parents and some teachers understand the critical nature of the second stage. Here are some proven methods to get the kid back on task.

ONE   Say to Dennis: "I know these are very challenging to you. I will do the first one and you will check my work. You will do the second and I will check your work. When we finish ten, we go for an ice cream cone. Whoever has the most problems correct gets treated. The one with the most mistakes pays."

Comment: I almost heard you picking apart this suggestion. You said as you read it, "I tried that one. It didn't work. My Dennis didn't have any money." Or you said, "What if I can't do the problem either?" or you said, "Swell idea, Dr. Zink. I have thiry-seven kids in my class. How can I do 185 problems (5 X 37) in the one hour I have of math." If you tore apart this idea as unworkable, I am not surprised that you have trouble motivating kids. Thinking negatively never motivated anyone to do much of anything. THINK POSITIVELY. Remember, negative thinking is why the kid is stuck at the second stage of the motivation cycle in the first place. Instead of picking apart my suggestion (that is all it was, really) Think: how can I **adapt** this idea to get my "Dennis" back on task? How can I make this idea **pay-off** for me? Now, partner, you're **thinking**.

TWO   "Caitrin, I am really impressed by how hard you are working. For every problem you get correct on your homework tonight, I will give you fifty cents! **However**, this money can **only** be used for **taking me** out to dinner at MacDonald's tonight. If you don't have at least five dollars, that's ten problems correct, we can't go. So let's get started! I am hungry and I can't wait to put my teeth into a BIG MAC! Come on, Caiti! Ronald MacDonald is waiting!

Comment: Remember the **most powerful** motivators for kids are **not** earning something for themselves, but **earning** something for someone they love, so give them a chance!

The Third Stage in the motivation cycle for kids is called "Review." This stage is the most critical of all. Children who are highly motivated periodically take stock of what they have accomplished. Children who are not motivated only can see how much remains to be done. And it often overwhelms them. It is a curious anomaly of human behavior, but it is true: people who are very successful will often take their eyes **off** the goal in order to review what they have accomplished. This is very true of successful young people. As a parent and teacher, you can put the principle of "Review" to work for you immediately. Kids who are stopped in the middle of a task may be stuck because as they work they realize how much more there is to do than **they originally suspected**. In other words, they are stalled at the second stage of the cycle, recognition. Kids who take apart toys, machines, clocks, and everything else mechanical and **never put them back together** are stuck at the recognition stage. The mini-bike is in 1000 pieces all over the garage floor because taking the bike apart is one-third or one-fourth of the total labor in the project, not one-half as your fifteen year old originally suspected.

You can get the project moving along by helping the young man (it is a rare young woman who will tackle mini-bike repair, but **it does happen**—I freely acknowledge this here to save you writing a steamy letter to me) realize that he has **accomplished** much already. Getting him to look over his work with a sense of **having done something** often will give him a sense of his place in the continuum of the project. A conversation might go like this:

FATHER: How's the mini-bike repair coming?

SON: Slowly. I got it apart but there's more work than I first thought. That transmission is real tricky.

FATHER: I bet. It is a machine within a machine.

SON: You got that right. I'm discouraged.

FATHER: I realize there is more to do than you first thought, but consider how much you have accomplished. I am amazed at how quickly you took it apart. If you were doing that job for someone else and charging them by the day, you'd be money ahead if you allowed for a day to take it apart. It only took you a few hours.

SON: I guess you're right. I didn't think of it that way. All I can see is that transmission and all those gears . . .

FATHER: Stay with it, partner. The job can be done with patience and you are the man to do it. If you get it together by Saturday, and I can have my garage back, we'll spend Saturday morning riding the bikes in the mountains. DEAL?

SON: Deal!

Compare the clever father above with the one below:

FATHER: I am sick and tired of leaving my car outside because my son's god damned mini-bike is strewn all over the garage that I pay for every month!

The Fourth Stage in the motivation cycle is called

Rededication. Rededication occurs when the kid realizes where she/he is on the continuum of a project and makes certain course corrections to insure that the project gets completed on the revised schedule to meet revised goals. It is at this stage that a kid's values on a particular project can be clarified and the remaining complex steps can be divided into simple ones. Here is the place to teach the difference between doing a task and doing a task **well**. In fact, it is at this stage in the motivation cycle that your greatest teaching can be done. My own greatest teachers did their most outstanding work for me in this stage. They taught me to generate simple alternative solutions to tricky problems at this stage. They taught me how to manipulate the system to work **for** me rather than **against** me at this stage. They taught me how to shape the tasks ahead to my strengths not my weaknesses as a student. They taught me how to make one interest count for many goals. They taught me to focus the energies I had on the task for the purpose of **doing a good job** rather than just getting the job done. In the rededication stage, which is the most creative stage of the motivational cycle, kids **explode** with enthusiasm. They find the freedom to experiment a wonderful and "earned" high. At this stage, they clean the room **better** than you do, they stay up all night writing a new computer program, painting the set for the class play, drafting an equation to represent the time-distance warp inside a black hole in space, or composing their own fugues on moog-synthesizers, which they built, of course. This is when they amaze you by rebuilding the '57 chevy with a high riser intake manifold, a competition clutch, a spring-loaded gear box, and a Holley 4500 carburetor rejetted to fit the '57 block.

At the rededication stage, it is important for parents and teachers to help the kids avoid certain pitfalls. Here they are:

ONE　　　Kids in the rededication stage believe they can **only** do what they do best; they will resist entering into the "RISK" or first stage of a new skill or task. Point out to them that anyone who can shoot a basketball at an iron ring 10 feet off the ground for six hours **without** stopping, **can** for one hour, study a play by William Shakespeare. Say that any child who can sit, mesmerized, in front of **Superfriends** on Saturday morning television for one solid hour, **can** sit still and listen or read during reading group at school. Any teenage girl who can memorize the words to all the cheers, the alma mater, the fight song, and 44 friends' telephone numbers, **can** memorize "How do I love Thee" by Elizabeth Barrett Browning. The rededication stage **is** the time and place to point out what they have mastered (stage three: Review) can now be applied to other new skills and tasks.

TWO　　　Another pitfall of the rededication stage for kids is burnout and exhaustion. In the exhilaration of the quest for self-discovery, they will override the normal biological warning signs from their minds and bodies. They will push themselves to superhuman effort and take dangerous health risks. Football players will resort to drugs at this stage. Anorexics will literally destroy themselves with the discovery of the social power they possess by refusing to eat. Skiers will do dare devil stunts ignoring potential serious consequences and students will take "uppers" to stay awake for days to cram for finals.

Parents who see their children in this stage often wonder out loud, "My God, I thought we'd never get him going; now, I wonder if we'll ever slow him down."

At this point a discussion of the fifth and final stage of the motivation cycle is quite appropriate because truly gifted and wise parents and teachers realize that the fifth stage is the best solution to the dangers of the fourth stage, rededication.

The final stage of the five stage cycle is called Readjustment. Readjustment takes place when kids learn how to pace themselves and work and play in moderation. The old Roman philosophers called this the **VIA MEDIA** and it means literally, the middle road. The greatest teacher I ever met, Dr. Lawrence N. Canjar, who before his death, was the Dean of the College of Engineering at the University of Detroit, once said to me in a private and revealing conversation. *"There have been times in my life when I really worked very hard. I bounded out of bed, in the saddle already, and* *worked all day and all night on the book (On Thermodynamics); then there were times when I was out of the saddle and wasted days and did nothing. This bothered me. I felt unproductive. Now I realize that these 'unproductive' times are quite important. They gave me the opportunity to rest and to* **readjust** *my goals and objectives. I realize now these periods of readjustment often preceeded my greatest work."* Readjustment is the process by which one decides which new directions to take and which new skills to learn. Parents and teachers who understand the readjustment phase of the motivation cycle are not overly concerned about listlessness after certain kids have completed sucessfully some task or mastered a new skill. Also, they understand motivation as a cycle: Risk, Recognition, Review, Rededication, and Readjustment. After Readjustment comes a new risk and the process begins anew. Students who fully understand the motivation cycle and how it works in them become life-long learners. These people are the most valuable people a society can produce. They cannot become obsolete because they always remain open to the possibility of a new cycle. Children who learn this lesson of the cycle early have a true gift. It is called security.

NOTES

NOTES

Chapter Three:

MONEY AND THE ZINK MONEY SYSTEM

The key to motivating youngsters is work. Keep them busy. Remember, the less time they have for trouble, the less trouble they will find. The best system I know for keeping them busy is outlined below. Follow these guidelines carefully. The Zink Money System for kids works best with ages 8 through 18, but I know parents who have adapted it successfully for kids 5, 6, and 7.

ONE   Divide the household chores and work into two categories. Call them category 'A' and category 'B' chores. Examples of category 'A' chores would be those chores which you expect the kids to do, **without pay**, because they are members of your household. These could include making the bed, picking up the room, cleaning the closet, emptying the trash, feeding the dog, etc. Category 'A' chores are done automatically—and consistently **praised,** do not forget, but kids are not paid for doing them. Paying a child to brush his or her teeth is ridiculous. However, if they **do not do** category 'A' chores, then they have chosen to **lose the right** to do category 'B' chores.

TWO   Category 'B' chores are those chores which parents would consider hiring someone to do—if they had no children to do them. Examples of category 'B' chores include washing the family cars, washing the windows, raking leaves and weeding or tilling the garden. Painting walls or trim work, scrubbing walls, washing floors, cleaning carpets, cutting grass, and babysitting are all reasonable examples of category 'B' chores. I am sure you can think of plenty of others and if you can't, ask the kids and they will help you. The point is this: After category 'A' chores are completed to your satisfaction, they may do category 'B' chores for **money**. But read on carefully.

THREE   Never give kids an allowance. Never. In case you did not hear me, I said "NEVER." Allowances breed two things: (1) fights and arguments; (2) welfare mentality. In the allowance system they show up on Friday with hand extended saying "Where's my five bucks?"

You say "But you did not clean the garage!"

They say, "But I did clean the bathroom. You're not fair!"

"I'm not fair? You did not live up to the terms of our agreement."

"But I need the money for the skateboard park. . ."

And so it goes.

Point two. Kids who get their money automatically (because after awhile it is easier to pay than fight with them) assume that the world owes them a living. Keep it up and you'll make his car payment for him when he's thirty-five years old.

FOUR Pay your kids a reasonable, **fair** rate **by the hour**. Don't rip off your kids and they will not rip you off. Fifty cents an hour is unrealistic. They are not stupid. They will not work for low wages because they have to live in the same economic world that we do. You set your own rate but if you err, err on the high side. Now before you throw down the book and say Dr. Zink doesn't live in the real world—where am I going to get all this money? Freeze and listen to me. All good employers have budgets. If you can only afford to employ your kids 3 or 4 hours a week at 3 or 4 dollars an hour, fine. Tell them in advance. Say, "Michael, this week you can work a total of 4 hours at category 'B' chores. I will pay you Friday." If Michael needs more money, let him work for the neighbors. They need painting work, garden work, and babysitting, too.

FIVE   Kids keep track of their own hours. I did not design this system to make a secretary of you for your children. Each kid gets his/her own stenographer's notebook. Four columns will do nicely. Date, chore, time, and total money amount. Tell Devon, "You are in charge of your own chore book. You keep track of the hours and the money I owe you. If you do a good job, you will receive three dollars an hour for each hour worked. If you do a poor job, I will not pay you. So, do a good job.* Also, never cheat me on the hours. If you do, I will only pay you two dollars an hour in the future. And if you cheat again, one dollar an hour. Also, keep your book up to date. I can call for it anytime. If it is up-to-date, when I ask to see it, you will receive a three dollar bonus. If it is not up-to-date when I ask to see it, there is a three dollar fine."

*Do not forget to **teach** the kids how to do the specifics of the task. Always breakdown new tasks into the individual skills involved and **take the time** to teach them how to do the job right. Because you pay by the hour, they are under pressure to do the job correctly, not just do it to get it done.

SIX.   Generously praise the work done by the kids. Do not assume that the money is the primary motivator. **It is not**. The excitement you feel when you see the kids do a good job should be communicated clearly and often. Also let them know how greatly you appreciate the help they are giving the family. If the work is not up to your standards, say so. But don't dwell on it. Say "Aaron, the windows are not clean enough. You must change the cleaning cloth more often, or use fresh newsprint and more windex. Remember to clean the corners. Those are the true test of a clean window. Start your time over and do them right. I know you can do a sensational job!"

SEVEN   Guideline seven concerns credit. You will be amazed at how well it works, but follow this guideline carefully or you will be in trouble. There are times when the kids just have to have something. You know this time. They get the desperate look on their faces which says they will die absolutely if they do not have a Sony Walkman II.

Like fresh air, pure water, and good food, a Walkman II complete with a Joan Jett tape and earphones is essential to life on the planet earth.

When this time comes most parents prepare themselves for the battle. "Eighty bucks? Is it made of gold? Your mother and I paid less than that for rent in 1964!"

Credit works like this. You advance them all or part of the money for the purchase. You **do not do** this if you are dead set against the purchase **or** if you are not certain how monies advanced will be used.

Next, you specify a reasonable (but not overly generous) time period for the repayment of the debt. You may even set a repayment schedule. For example, a fourteen-year old boy who is advanced eighty dollars for a Walkman II, and who spends much of his time either in school or doing his homework, can be expected to repay the debt in **one month** if he is paid four dollars an hour. This means he must find twenty hours during four weekends to work off his debt. This is reasonable.

However, you must specify some conditions to him. 1) If he fails to repay the debt in the specified time, he will not be extended credit in the future. 2) If he does repay the debt in the specified time, not only will he have further opportunities for credit, but his credit limit will be extended to 100 or 125 dollars next time. (Or as you can afford it.)

Futhermore, this condition will arise: while he is paying off his debt, a need for pocket money may develop. When this happens, I recommend you **split wages** with him.

Here is how splitting works: if he is paid four dollars an hour, he deducts from his debt two dollars for every hour he works and is paid two dollars in cash for each hour. This will keep money in his pocket and steadily reduce his debt.

EIGHT Remember that the main purpose of the Zink Money System is to teach responsibility to youngsters. It helps them feel good about themselves for accomplishing something. Instead of whining and wishing and moping for something they want, the system teaches them they can have anything they are willing to work hard for. Consider what holding their hands out for money all the time does to their self-respect and self-image. Our job is not to make beggars of our children but to teach them to be self-reliant. The Zink Money System also has a profound effect on the ways kids treat their possessions. A kid who spends twenty hours washing cars and windows and cutting grass to earn his Sony Walkman II will think twice about abusing it. So, do not play catch-22 with the kids. The whole idea is **not** for you to keep changing the ground rules so they can't win. The whole idea will smack you in the face with its effectiveness, when the two of you get in the car and drive to the store. There, in the seat next to you, he sits with his hard earned money (or brand new debt!) in his pocket and you see the look on his face when he puts the money in the store clerk's hands. What you have taught him is how to make the world meet his needs in a friendly, honest, and fair fashion. So you want the kids to win. Winning builds confidence that they can win again. Please shout and make noise when the last dollar on the debt is paid. Remember how good you felt when you ripped the last car payment coupon out of the book and wrote the last check.

NINE Now that your kid has earned something and has experienced the growth of working for and achieving something, you are in an excellent position to protect that growth. This is done with rules and consequences. For example, when my son Joe was nine he worked for twenty-five hours at a wage of three dollars an hour to earn the money to buy the most expensive and beautiful skateboard in Dewey Weber's Surfshop on the Pacific Coast Highway in Redondo Beach. I was there to watch him put the seventy-five dollars in the hands of old Dewey, himself. On the way home Joe and I had a chat because I saw him with his arms wrapped around that shiny skateboard and I had this mental flash of the pain he would experience if someone stole it.

So, rather than lecture, I made a rule. If the skateboard is left outside, unattended, it is gone for 3 days.

It goes in my closet, in my bedroom, and **no plea bargaining**. Of course, after I told Joe the rule and the consequence for breaking it, I asked him to repeat it. Competent teachers and knowledgable parents always have the kids repeat directions to insure that the message has been received. This affords the opportunity to respond with a positive message when they repeat the direction correctly. It is so easy to say, "You got it, partner. Thank you for listening so carefully." Joe had to put the skateboard in my closet once. It happened 10 days after our drive home. I came home from a lecture I had given, saw the skateboard in the front yard, and didn't see Joe. I walked into the house with the board in my hand and he came flying out of his room.

He looked at me, looked at the skateboard, and said, "How was your day?"

I said, "Great day. How was yours?"

"Fine. Until now."

Then, with a brightening of his eyes he said, "I bet they loved your workshop!"

"They did, Joe. And I need a shower because I'm out of steam."

I leaned the board carefully against

the living room wall. By the time I was in the shower, the board was in my closet, in my bedroom, where it remained entombed for three days. One of those days was the skateboard park challenge race day and Joe did not participate. No words were spoken on the subject then; and to date we have never discussed it. That happened five years ago and Joe has not left his skateboard or anything else outside unattended since. Of course, his mother and I always make a point of telling him how proud we are that he takes good care of his possessions.

Quintessentially, this story illustrates the Zink method at its most powerful best. There **is no reason** why you cannot use the same method with great success with your children. Let me repeat with stronger emphasis: **There is absolutely no reason whatsoever that this approach will not work for you**. Remember kids know that talk is cheap. Action gets results.

NOTES

Chapter Four:

GRADES AND THE ZINK CHART

The Zink Chart is a system for tracking a kid's progress in school. The chart belongs on the back of the kid's bedroom door (doors are large enough to accommodate several charts if the bedrooms are multi-occupied). This position affords semi-privacy. A kid who wants his or her chart unobserved keeps the door open. If the grades are low, you want that door open, anyway. It is important to observe what is and what is not being accomplished in that room. Stiff cardboard makes a good chart.* Across the top of the chart are the days of the school year. Down the left hand side are the individual academic subjects. The boxes caused by the intersecting lines are for recording grades received on papers, drawings, book reports, quizzes, tests, etc. Letter grades are recorded in black ink. B, C+, C−, etc. The letter grade A is **not** recorded. Instead, a red bullseye is drawn in the box. These can be seen from as far as across the room and they have maximum visual and psychological impact. Some parents allow their children to tape or thumbtack a large manila envelope under the chart to hold all school papers for the current school term. The wisest of parents challenge their children to score bullseyes and reward the accumulation of these with special desserts, trips to the ice cream store, or special articles of clothing (with little alligators on them, of course).

*Author's Note: A laminated and reusable, deluxe version of the Zink Chart can be purchased from J. Zink, Inc., P.O. Box 3279, Manhattan Beach, California, 90266, for 9.95 plus 1.50 postage and handling.
CA residents add 6.5 percent.

The key to the Zink Chart magic is the enthusiasm parents generate for obvious progress.

Progress is one predictable outcome for the child using a Zink Chart. Remember the kid's name should be on the chart's top in bold letters. It is a good idea to put the name of the school, the teacher's name(s), and any other pertinent remarks like "GO GET 'EM, BULLSEYES!"

Kids who use the Zink Chart are given a way to watch their progress in school; after a few weeks, a pattern will develop naturally. This pattern will help parents determine which subjects need work **before** the dreaded report card comes home. Also, when the report card does arrive, there will be no awful surprises. These awful surprises make for terrible scenes, tears, thunderous pronouncements, and ominous bad feelings. These doom-filled report card days can destroy that part of a child's self-concept which pertains to school, studies, and formal academic self-development. At the very least, the Zink Chart prevents the bad surprise and softens the destructive aspects of strong parental disappointment. At very best, parents find their children challenged by the visual proof of their academic labors. My own son, using a chart, once recorded twenty-three bullseyes in a row. When I asked him why he did so spectacularly well, he said, "I decided that a B would be embarrassing."

And now a word of caution about the Zink Chart. It will lose its impact if you let it. So, instead of asking the age-old "What did you learn in school today?" You can watch while he/she records the day's achievements. This will afford you a multiplicity of opportunities to discuss various strategies for grade improvement and study skill development. It will be the place for generating a plan of action.

In lower grades or ungraded circumstances, verbal comments made by the child's teacher can be recorded in the appropriate spaces. Also, some parents use the bottom of each subject space to help the student keep track of long term assignments. This tracking avoids another painful scene: The discovery at dinner the night before that tomorrow the nine weeks' project is due. . .

A FINAL WORD OF WARNING:

Don't let several days of grades go unrecorded. Especially for grade-school students. It becomes too large a job to wade through large stacks of papers, so the grades go unrecorded. Also, it is natural for kids to be quick to record good grades and slow to record less outstanding ones, so be sure **all** grades are recorded every night. The way to insure that **all** grades are recorded is to drop a note to your child's teacher requesting that you be notified **every** time he/she receives a grade lower than a C. Some clever parents give the teacher stamped and pre-addressed envelopes for this purpose. Others provide work and home phone numbers and praise **heavily** the teacher for taking the time to call. Also, let your son or daughter **know** that the teacher(s) will call or write with notice of a poor performance. This will stop the old "Oh, **that** test!"

NOTES

Chapter Five:

FRIENDS AND HOW TO TEACH
KIDS TO CHOOSE GOOD ONES

One of the most perplexing problems for today's parents is deciding what to do about their children's friends. When our children are small, we encourage them to develop friendships and good social skills because we know the importance of these skills throughout their lives. Yet, when our older children pick friends and come under their influence, we are generally frightened or intimidated because it seems that we have no control over their behavior.

It is important to recognize that peer pressure, peer approval, and the need for peer acceptance are powerful forces in the lives of our kids. Unfortunately, peers often encourage and reward the wrong behavior in our children. Perhaps you have participated in or have observed an episode like the following: Mother says to daughter, "You were caught doing what? Shoplifting? Oh, my God, I don't believe this! You were with that Smith girl, weren't you? I told you she was bad news, didn't I?"

This mother's response to the alleged influence of the Smith girl on her daughter is typical. What is also typical is that this mother had probably never spent the time to have a plainly instructive chat with her daughter about what to look for in choosing a friend. As with most parents, she reacted instead to her daughter's choice of a friend after the friendship was already established.

Unfortunately, most parents fail to recognize that there are many things they can do to enhance the quality of their children's friendships. Rather than being threatened by the growing attachment of their child to the peer group, they must begin to understand that kids of all ages have strong social needs and must get these needs met in order to be happy. They also should understand that it is absolutely necessary for parents to assist their children to develop the social skills they need for successful social living.

Until our kids learn certain "life" lessons, they will be prey to their needs for love, acceptance, and approval. For example, the world is filled with predators who either consciously or unwittingly destroy and hurt many of the people they touch. Is it not important for our kids to learn the difference between people who love you for what you are and people who pretend to love you because you can be used as an instrument in fulfilling their selfish goals and aspirations? Is it not important for our kids to learn the difference between people who are "givers" and people who are "takers," between people who are "helpers" and people who are "users"?

What this boils down to is the fact that there is a particularly critical skill our children must have if they are to successfully survive in today's world. The skill is **picking and choosing friends**.

Parents should also recognize that they can definitely influence their children's choice of friends as well as determine the quality of their relationships. The following four suggestions, for example, have proven most effective in helping parents in this most important area of parental guidance:

ONE   Watch for the behavior your children's friends encourage in your children;

watch for the behavior of your
children towards their friends.

It is easier to understand the motivating factors behind
your children's everyday decisions when you realize that
they are generally an integral part of a circle of friends and
acquaintances which has a behavior code and a value
orientation of its own. This code and orientation may embrace some of your own values, but they also could incor-
porate values that are foreign and threatening to your
own. Observing the messages that are sent to your
children by their friends will not only help you understand your children's behavior, but it will also help you
assess the major differences between "your world" and
"their world." Remember, if your children are to be happy
they will do so in their own world. In short, they must
follow the rules of their own world in order to survive
without serious scars, psychological traumas, or emotional
setbacks.

An important way to understand your children's world
is by being vigilant about the messages of mutual regard
that children exchange. If they reward one another for
wearing certain shirts, jeans, blouses, or shoes because
they happen to be "in," do not get upset but view the
situation as an opportunity to interact with them in a con-
structive way. Unfortunately, most parents fail to do so.
Because "in" clothes inevitably cost more, many parents
become outraged. "Why should I pay $21.95 for this
because it has that silly logo, when I can buy the same
thing at K-Mart for $8.95?"

This is not to suggest that parents should give in on

every issue and turn over the checkbook to the kid. Far from it. Understanding the circumstances behind the behavior, particularly those related to peer presure, gives the parent excellent opportunity to build a positive self-concept in the youngster. Witness: "Jeffrey, I understand the situation. All your friends wear brand name shirts. You like them too. But they cost six and a half dollars more than a similar shirt without the brand name. Here's the deal. I think you are number one, and you should wear the best. So, you'll have to earn the difference be-tween the cost of the two shirts. I'll pay two dollars an hour for window cleaning, leaf raking, and babysitting your brother and sister."

Now Jeffrey has the opportunity to wear the clothes he wants in order to feel comfortable among his friends. Fur-thermore, he has a great incentive to work! His shirts take on new meaning. They are now, at least partially, the pro-duct of his own labor. Do you think he will store them at the bottom of his closet all crumpled up like his other shirts? More than likely, you will find them neatly hung in a closet or folded carefully in his drawer. After all, he did spend his hard earned money to buy them!

We should also realize that Jeffrey's friends are not the only ones who are sending messages; for Jeffrey himself is also reciprocating with messages of his own. By watching those, you will learn an enormous amount not only about Jeffrey, but also about **yourself**. Is he mean to his friends? Is he moody with his friends? Does he tease them to the point of pain? Does he use them for his own ends? Whatever his attitude and messages, the probable fact is that a great deal of his behavior reflects what he learned from you.

TWO   Know your children's friends.

Go out of your way to closely associate with them, if only for brief but meaningfully shared experiences. Invite them to your parties, picnics, outings, camping trips, or simply to spend an hour or two with your children in your own home.

THREE   Do not cross-examine your children's friends.

If they suspect that they are invited for the purpose of scrutiny and information-gathering about themselves or their families, they will evaporate like dew on a warm desert morning. Questions like "What does your father do for a living?" may be harmless enough, but the game of "twenty-questions" grows very old with kids and they get a very negative message from the interrogation. Learn who they are by observing them and not by asking too many questions.

FOUR   Periodically, discuss your children's friends with your children.

One of the worst things you can do is to give your children the impression that you are the ultimate judge about the quality of their friendships. Do not do it! What you should strive for instead is for your son or daughter to acquire the skill of evaluating and of making their own decisions about his or her friends. Because friendships are so important to all of us, they should be treated with the utmost delicacy. Yes, we all believe it is a basic human right to choose our own friends, and in this respect children are no different.

A last tip before closing: Do not hesitate to point out the lovable qualities of your own friends to your children. You should realize that one of the most powerful ways to teach children how to develop warm, supportive, and lasting friendships is by discussing with them your reasons for loving, admiring, and supporting your friends.

In doing this, you give your children a special gift which will last a lifetime. You give them the gift of choosing and maintaining true friendships.

In order to help your children gain insights to the role of friendship in their lives, here is a friendship quiz for them to read and answer. There are no "right" and "wrong" answers to this quiz. The questions are designed to help kids recognize when friendship can cause them trouble and lead them to bad decisions. Effective parents and teachers have used this quiz as a study guide for generating meaningful discussions about the plus and minus views of human relationships.

THE FRIENDSHIP QUIZ

1)   Do you feel that you picked your friend or did he/she pick you?

2) What things do you and your friend have in common? Name at least three.

3) What do you usually disagree about?

4) Who usually wins these disagreements?

5) Does your friend get upset when other people join your group?

6) Does your friend ever say or do anything that frightens you?

7) Does your friend get into trouble more times or · fewer times at school than you do?

8) Does your friend get in trouble more times or fewer times at home than you do?

9) Do you like the way your friend treats his/her parents, brothers, and sisters?

10) What's the best time you've ever had with your friend and what's the worst time you've ever had with him/her?

NOTES

Chapter Six:

CLASSROOM DISCIPLINE AND THE CONFERENCE WITH THE TEACHER

We hear a lot these days on the subject of school discipline. We hear that the public **and** teachers think lack of school discipline is the number one problem facing American education. We read about teachers assaults, rapes at school, even school murders in the newspapers. But it all comes home the day the phone rings and Michael's teacher is requesting a conference to discuss Michael's behavior at school. She tells you that in addition to missing several key assignments, Michael's attention span has been remarkably short and now he is stopping some of the other children from doing their schoolwork. It is in Michael's best interest, she says, that you and perhaps your husband (if he's available, she adds) meet with her tomorrow after school to discuss Michael's behavior.

You thank her for her concern and agree on a 3:30 meeting in her classroom, replace the phone, gulp, and resist the urge to A) make yourself a drink, B) call your mother, C) call your husband even though you have not talked for two months, D) call your girlfriend—because she will tell you ad nauseam how bad her kids are. Biting your lip, you get that tightness in your stomach that remembers your own unhappiest moments in school. But you are embarrassed, so with quiet resolve, you plot the murder of your first-born. Ten minutes later, Michael walks in the door and knows immediately that something is amiss; what's this? no milk and cookies? And the shadow of the hangman's noose on the front door says "I'm in trouble!"

A more positive approach might include a statement like this: "Michael, Mrs. Davis called me today to discuss your behavior in her class. She said you are leaving your seat without her permission and you are stopping her from teaching. She also said you are disrupting other children who are trying to learn. What do you have to say about this?"

"Aw, Mom. Billy Maxwell and Bobby Jarrett are always getting me in trouble. Mrs. Davis never sees them. Just me. She hates me."

"We have an appointment with Mrs. Davis tomorrow after school. At that time we will come up with a plan to deal with this problem. For now, get to your homework."

Here are some guidelines to make meeting Michael's teacher pleasant and productive; following these will be a few suggestions for helping Michael develop a positive self-concept which **include** feeling good about himself for doing his assignments and not disrupting other children at work.

1) When you sit down with Michael's teacher, be pleasant, courteous, and avoid being defensive. Even if the kid she describes does not sound like Michael, do not say "I'm sorry, but the child you're describing does not sound like my Michael." Instead, thank her for her concern and professional interest in Michael. Remember, a teacher who requests a conference on discipline **is a rare teacher**. Most teachers are so punished by the thought of a parent conference, they ignore the problem and may ignore the kid as well.

2) Be positive in your discussion of Michael and his performance. Focusing on the negative aspects of

Michael's behavior may serve to reinforce his teacher's low expectations of Michael's ability to achieve.

For example, you can say: "Mrs. Davis, I appreciate your concern for Michael. I am very proud of the way he behaves at home. So I know he is capable of controlling his behavior."

3) Insist that Michael's teacher give you specific problem areas and stress your willingness to assist her (him) in encouraging Michael to improve his performance in these areas.

For instance, if Mrs. Davis says "I just don't know what to do with him sometimes!," You can say, "I understand. Now what specific things does he do so we can make some rules, and consequences for not following them. Also, we can come up with some pleasant things to occur when he does follow them!"

4) In other words, the **real purpose** of your visit with Michael's teacher is to develop **a plan of action**. This plan should be very simple but include the following items: A) Specific areas of improvement such as assignments done on time, working on his own at school, etc. B) What both of you will do if Michael shows no improvement **in the next few days**, such as loss of privileges for Michael, another conference with Michael present, etc. C) What both of you will do if Michael shows improvement **in the next few days**, including specific praise, a special privilege, etc. It is a very good idea to write these items down to formalize your mutual plan of action. Michael's teacher will be very impressed that you care enough about

her to record your agreement about Michael **on paper**. Remember, most teachers have **no formal training** in the area of classroom discipline. As incredible as that sounds, it is true. Michael's need of self-control will never be served if you walk into your meeting with his teacher with an attitude which says, "If you can't handle this little problem, how come you are in this profession?"

5) Promise Michael's teacher that you will support her (his) efforts to motivate Michael.

If Michael has the grace to thank his teacher as you leave, remember to tell him on the way home **how well** he handled himself at the meeting. Tell him that you are confident that he can improve his behavior and it is a good idea to sweeten the deal at this point. Tell him that five days **in a row** with no trouble at school means a celebration dinner at his favorite restaurant.

6) Do not "interrogate" Michael when he comes home from school the next day. If he has a note from his teacher which praises his work that day, put the note on the refrigerator, or some other prominent place of display, and send a copy of the note to Michael's grandparents. They will praise him plenty for good behavior. What you want Michael to learn is this: **He gets all the attention he needs by behaving himself**. And if he doesn't, get busy!

Some parents play "something good/something bad" and it avoids the old what-did-you-do-at-school-today question. At the end of each school day, or at an appropriate time, the parent says "something good" and Michael tells of **one** good thing that happened to him that day. Then "something bad" tells about something that he didn't like. It is a natural avenue for him to vent his feelings and/or relieve himself of some guilt over an incident that needs sharing with a parent. Parents who focus only on the "something bad" quickly teach their youngsters that their only interest is in what went wrong rather than what went right. The trick is to focus on the good things while permitting the child to share any setbacks and discuss them quietly and without intense emotion.

Some parents often add "What do you wish had happened today?" This teaches children how to visualize positive outcomes and is a very important skill in the development of a positive self-concept.

7) Keep in touch with Michael's teacher over the course of the year. Even if the problem is completely solved, it is a very good idea to periodically check with Michael's teacher on his progress in other areas. Teachers often admit that they try ever so much harder with a child whose parents have expressed repeatedly their concern for and intent to support a quality education for their children. An old fashioned idea, but one whose time has come again: invite Michael's teacher to Sunday dinner. She (he) will love the special treatment! And the teacher will get an opportunity to see the Michael you know and love.

NOTES

Chapter Seven:

FOOD AND HOW TO HELP KIDS EAT RIGHT

Motivating youngsters to eat food which is good for them is easy when you follow a few simple guidelines.

ONE   Like other aspects of the Zink method for discipline, getting good food into your kids involves making the right choices. So give them a choice. Instead of asking "How about some asparagus, partner?" To which the answer they give is "No!," Say "Meagan, the choice is yours, asparagus with yummy melted cheese like pizza, **or** broccoli salad with those cute little chick peas on top?"

TWO   Blend in good ingredients to dishes which are established favorites with your children. Whole-wheat, oatmeal, soy flour, or grated carrots can be added to breads and pizza crust. Peas, broccoli, and spinach can be chopped, grated, or pureed and added to stews and soups.

THREE   Don't suddenly announce "There is going to be a new regime around here. No more sweets, no more preservatives, no more etc." Quietly and efficiently remove one item at a time from your usual diet, and substitute—one at a time—a more healthy and nutritious food. You can, over the course of six months achieve

all of your food goals for your family and do it with no fighting.

FOUR   Don't fight at dinnertime. It is very unhealthy and terribly tiring. It takes 30% of your body's total energy to digest a stomach full of food. If you must battle (you do not **have** to fight, you know; it is usually a bad choice) do so when you can devote **all** of your resources to it. Do not play brinksmanship with kids over carrots; carrots are not that important. Kids feelings are important. But don't let them substitute Milk Duds for carrots, either. Just give them larger helpings of the **good** food they do like.

FIVE   Best suggestion of all. Give your kids responsibility for making part of the meal. This could be an "A" or "B" chore, (see Chapter Three on the Zink Money System) but the powerful psychological effect of food preparation practically **guarantees** they will eat what they help prepare. Of course, the praise they receive at mealtime will become an effective positive message and soon they will be in the kitchen, by demand, making their "specialty," which has become a family favorite. Special Hint: Don't permit them to make the same old thing.

Encourage them to experiment and **give them** the task of "hiding" nutritious food in old favorites. You will be amazed at the creativity kids bring to food preparation and, of course, you will have less work. **Further Hint**: Don't keep your boys out of the kitchen because they are boys. Boys in the kitchen are in training for a liberated marriage and, most of the great chefs of the world are still men. N'est ce-pas?

SIX Don't push food on kids. They need much less food than you think they need. You feel guilty when you see their thin little bodies, I know. You think "I am a bad parent and a rotten cook and provider because they just sit there and pick. He pushes the food around his plate and hardly touches it. She says "I'm not feeling very well" everytime we sit down to eat. If these statements sound familiar, relax. Just wait until they are teenagers and you do not dare stand between them and the refrigerator. It can be more dangerous than the freeway.

SEVEN If they want to snack, let them snack on fruit or raw vegetables. Actually, these snacks are better for them than most full course meals—particularly those with red meat. So keep the candy and other sweets **out of the house**. Do not buy or let them buy **anything** with sugar, additives, preservatives, or food dyes in them. Fill the cookie jar with figs and dates. Fill the candy bowl with fruit. If you can ween them away from sugar for one month, the battle is won, because after a month, sugar will no longer taste good to them. When they ask for Twinkies at the store, it's probably going to lead to a fight when you say "No." I've talked to parents who refuse to take their kids with them to food shop because of these scenes. This solution is not practical for many and may, by removing the opportunity for their input into the foods chosen, lead to the mini-mart raids so many kids make these days.

Instead, the grocery store is a great place to teach kids about what you **mean** by good foods. To avoid scenes and help kids choose good food, you might try this approach.

1) Before you go to the store, share with the kids what you need to buy. They usually know the cupboard supply better than you do.

2) Tell them before they enter the

store that they may choose a certain number of items (you pick the number), **but** you must approve these items. This not only gives them a part in the choices but keeps them occupied. Remember, the grocery store is boring if all you can do there is push the cart or worse, sit in it.

3) Certain items can be listed as "off-limits" to avoid the weekly fight. For example, **nothing** may be chosen from the packaged cookie shelves. Also, since supermarkets stock many non-food impulse-purchase items such as toys, magazines, and clothes, you might want to exclude these as appropriate choices in advance.

You may get surprised when the kids make their choices. They will not always pick junk food. Their choices may include a brand of pickles you typically do not purchase because of outrageous prices, special lunch meat, fancy juices in high-tech cardboard boxes, or "Homemade" pizza for dinner.

4) Involve kids in the other choices which must be made in the supermarket. Apple or orange juice wheat or rye bread (with the little seeds!),

pork or lamb chops, etc. Give them
responsibility and they will love you
for it!

A special note for working mothers (who always feel guilty!):

You **can** control the foods your children eat even if you
are not there to monitor after school snacking. Have
nutritious foods prepared and ready to eat. A child may
pass up an orange because it is not quartered in favor of
something less healthy but more accessible.

Have celery in the refigerator; fill the celery with cheese
or peanut butter; replace chips with popcorn or crackers;
have hard-boiled eggs waiting in a bowl; or put tooth
picks in pieces of cheese or pickles.

Remember the largest source of sugar in your child's
diet is probably not candy or cookies. **It is sugar cereal**.
Do not relent on your brave stance **not** to purchase what
is advertised on Saturday morning cartoon commercials.

Kids usually eat **tons** of cereal while growing so your
time spent in the cereal aisle is very important.

I personally believe that a special place in the inferno is
reserved for those who make a living selling sugar cereal
to children. Take that, CAPTAIN CRUNCHO!

NOTES

Chapter Eight:

VIDEO ARCADES AND HOW TO STOP VIDIOTS

There can be little doubt that the video arcades of today are what pool halls were to a previous generation: A place to waste time. They go beyond the bounds of recreation for most kids. Video arcades are a world unto themselves. With realistic sound tracks for excitement and an eyeball dazzling display of simulated violence, they snag youngsters into cheap accomplishments. Video machines swallow quarters in exchange for immortalization on the screen: Gia scored 23,474 points for this week's all time high.

Not that the video games do not give kids skills. I would have better understood Luke Skywalker's remarkable ability to handle a star fighter if I had seen a video game in his uncle's house. Fine motor skills, visual perception, hand-eye coordination and auditory learning are all delightful outcomes of the video game experience for kids. With increased reaction times, they will be better automobile drivers. It has been remarked, no doubt with some truth, that we are raising a generation of fighter pilots. It is a most appropriate remark, since real fighter pilots play those games incessantly to pass the time and sharpen their skills.

Also, as one pilot friend of mine who teaches flying in a flight simulator said with great insight, "No one ever got killed flying a simulator."

Which brings me to the most unhappy aspect of the VIDEO GAME REVOLUTION: It is a hollow and thoroughly unproductive experience **in the long run** for our kids. Worse, it is essentially violent. There is no time to negotiate with the Space Invaders. Shoot to kill or be blown to bits along with your quarter. After one learns this lesson (takes one quarter) **and** after one masters pressing the **fire** button, squeezing the trigger, rotating the warship, slamming the force field, avoiding the mountain, and lazering the omicrons to iddy biddy vidicrons, the experience is over. But the danger persists. Here are some reasons why parents and teachers should take steps to **limit** the time youngsters spend in the video arcades.

ONE   They are breeding grounds for drugs. When the pushers get thrown off the school campuses, they head for the one other place sure to be filled with kids. VIDEOLAND.

TWO   In many states the video games can be found in bars and liquor stores. (Very hard to find them in churches.)

THREE   The video addicts are addictive personalities, of course. Addictive personalities are not known for a high interest in personal growth: They are known for a high interest in **Gambling**.

FOUR   It takes money to feed the video monster. Depending on his/her (don't count out girls—they are often the best players) skill level, a kid can go through five to ten dollars in less than an hour. At the ten dollar rate a kid playing only ten hours a week can go through $5200 a year! Now you see why those machines are everywhere. Forget about what they do to our kids; as J. R. says, "Money is Money."

FIVE Kids who are not independently wealthy will have to work or steal to support their video habit. Here is an even money bet: Kids who have to work for their money loath to see it disappear **faster than they can make it**. So, odds are high that the kids are feeding the video monster with money they begged, borrowed, or stole from you. Or someone else.

Quickest cure for children afflicted with seemingly terminal VIDIOTICS:

Dr. Zink's Money System (see chapter on the Zink Money System). This system cures the video game blues in three dramatic ways. 1) It insures that the kids **work** for their money; 2) The more they work, the less time they have for the arcade; and 3) Kids who work under this system develop a strong sense of self-esteem. These kids are not easily found wasting great blocks of time in the video arcades of America.

There is one other effective method for combating the arcade blues. At the same time you **forbid** your youngster to frequent these places, install (or have him/her buy, which is much better) **your own** video game system in your home.

Now it is where you can legislate its use and make it dependent on kept promises regarding study hours, improved grades, observed house rules, etc.

One other advantage becomes apparent when the system is in your own home: Now you can join in the fun. "Kid, I've been from one end of this galaxy. . ."

NOTES

Part Three:

OUT OF CONTROL
AND
STEPS TO TAKE NOW

And they were bringing little children to him that he might touch them; but the disciples rebuked those who brought them. But when Jesus saw them, he was indignant, and said to them, "Let the little children come to me, and do not hinder them, for such is the Kingdom of God."

St. Mark
Chapter 10
Verses 13, 14

Chapter Nine:

ALCOHOL AND KIDS

Alcohol **is** in our culture. The question is: How do you introduce it into your child's life positively?

Today, alcohol is the drug of preference among kids. This is so because alcohol is easily obtained. Its use is condoned and even encouraged by our society. According to recent surveys among teen and pre-teen populations, more than 75% of today's youngsters drink alcoholic beverages **regularly** at parties. Wine and especially beer are the drugs of high use; occasionally hard liquor is the drug of choice. Kids today believe they cannot have fun at a gathering without alcohol. The problem is so widespread that in several recent studies teens and pre-teens estimate that up to fifteen percent of their friends have serious drinking problems and are, in fact, alcoholics.

The greatest frustration educators and concerned parents face in the drinking teen problem is the **source** of the alcohol. More than one-third of the teens and pre-teens in a recent California survey said their parents or their friends' parents supplied them with "all the alcohol they could drink."

Of course even without parent suppliers alcohol is ubiquitous at school events and community celebrations. Older brothers and sisters are often a source and, in some states, the local liquor or drug store delivers right to your home. Delivery personnel are loath to "make the trip for nothing," so checking identification has become passe'.

Finally, every community seems to have a bar or tavern, or worse, a **specific establishment** for the underaged, where alcohol is served **no questions asked**.

To parents worried about alcohol abuse among teens and pre-teens, witch hunts for suppliers are a waste of precious time. For every place of evil you attack like Carrie Nation with an axe, three will appear the next day. Here are some useful and time-productive suggestions for dealing **effectively** with alcohol use among youngsters.

ONE   Educate your children or students about the realities of alcohol so, when offered something stiff to drink, they can make an intelligent decision. This education includes a discussion of alcohol as a **mind altering substance** which, even in small quantities, can result in personal injury, intense suffering, and death. Tell them experts say fatal automobile accidents **more often than not** are caused by alcohol.

This education **includes** a frank and open discussion of the pain that alcohol causes to those who bury their dead alcoholic friends and relatives. Such a discussion should include a discussion of brain and liver damage which **always** results from alcohol use in even small amounts. Field trips to the local morgue and a talk with autopsy surgeons and pathologists are always instructive and sobering. Seeing the tissue damage which alcohol does to the human body is often a convincing lesson for the young.

Teachers who invite local psychologists, physicians, social workers, and other professionals who work with alcoholics to speak to their junior high school classes are reporting wonderful new attitudes toward drinking as a continuous life style. The local chapter of Alcoholics Anonymous will be delighted to provide speakers, **at no cost**, as part of your program.

Parents who find their children repeatedly drunk are having success at educating their children by taking them to Al-Anon. These meetings consist of support groups which share excellent information which teaches how to survive life with an alcoholic. As a side benefit, they provide excellent insight into the nightmare of alcoholism. Teens who attend one meeting report a dramatic reduction in drinking behavior.

TWO   As soon as they come home drunk, **do something about it**. Do not think of this behavior as a "stage" or something all kids have to go through. Valuable time can be lost in this "stage." **FACE FACTS**. Denial on the part of both the drinker and the family is one of the most destructive stages of alcoholism. Better to over-react to the problem than to wait and face the destruction of life, personality, health, and motivation. Many kids become addicted quite rapidly. It does not take **YEARS** of drinking.

So, take away privileges. Remove the telephone when you leave the house. Lock up his/her set of keys to your car. Lock up the keys to his/her car in your safety deposit box. Charge them rent or raise the rent if you already charge them. Fine them **big** dollars if you are using the

Zink Money System. Stop buying their favorite goodies at
the store. Stop the free ride service. Add more "A" chores
and household duties. Ground them. No friends over for
pajama parties. Put them on an airplane to visit Aunt Sally
for the week in Topeka (you know, Aunt Sally, she goes
to church **every** day) or do none of the above if you do
not like these suggestions, but **do something**. Your inac-
tivity when they lose control of themselves tells them **you
do not care**.

THREE   Immediately arrange for family
                counseling and go with them to **every**
                session. There are truly gifted and
                selfless, tireless workers out there who
                can help your youngster and you. If
                you do not love the first session or
                two, find someone else, but keep look-
                ing. Sometimes the process works in
                spite of itself. I have heard stories that
                the therapy sessions were such a turn-
                off to the kids, they struck a bargain:
                No more counseling and no more
                drinking. The parents responded by
                saying next time you drink we go back
                to the beard and the pipesmoke who
                says "How do **you** feel about that,
                Robbie?" Yuk.

FOUR   Look at your own drinking habits.
                How can you possibly expect kids to
                control their impulse to drink when
                you can't control yours? If you forget
                that alcohol is a **drug**, you can be sure

your teenagers will remind you. It is very possible to teach them to control their behavior by **deliberately** controlling yours.

FIVE   If all else fails, then **stop feeling guilty**. You did everything in your power to educate, help, and advise; now realize that they have the right to make bad decisions for which they choose to pay a very steep price. In the end, the truth is the only person you can totally control is **you**. Guilt is a terribly destructive human emotion. Get beyond guilt's corrosive grasp. Do something positive with all the energy you are using to abuse yourself.

SIX   It is a scientific fact that people with a history of alcoholism in their families (parents, grandparents, aunts, uncles) need to be more careful in their drinking habits.

If there is an alcohol-abuse history in your family, do not be afraid to share this information with your children.

What better example to show them than the drinking pattern of someone they know. All the better example, if the relative has dealt successfully with his/her alcohol problem.

A final few words on the teen drinking problem are in

---

order here. The **main thrust** of your attempt to help kids with alcohol should be to help them feel good about themselves **for not drinking**. So when they come home from a party and they are sober, it is cause for celebration. Let them catch your attention by demonstrating control not by losing it.

It is more than OK, it is wonderful when you can say, "Sandra, you cannot know how proud I am that you can go to a party with your friends and come home sober. I am a winner as a parent because you are a winner as a daughter and I thank God for you and I love you more than my words can express."

NOTES

Chapter Ten:

DRUGS AND KIDS

So much has happened in recent years to teach us all about the terrifying consequences of substance abuse among our young people. A great deal has been written concerning this serious social problem. For me to repeat here all these well-known warnings would be of little value. Even though alcohol is a drug, there remains a major difference between how certain parents and teachers view the use by young people of drugs and the use of alcohol. This attitudinal difference is worth our scrutiny.

While a great many parents and, suprisingly, many teachers accept the use of alcohol among the young as commonplace, few parents and teachers are willing to accept drug use in the young. There is an exception, of course, and that is marijuana. **Most** parents who discover marijuana use among their children react, after the shock, by mitigating the circumstance with a statement like "As long as he/she never tries anything stronger." And I have been a consultant to school districts, which shall go unnamed here, where the kids are so out-of-control, the teachers are happy the kids are stoned because they tend to be more manageable.

It is a serious **mistake** to mitigate the circumstance of marijuana use by saying it is ok as long as they don't do anything stronger. Because as a parent and teacher you must realize that A) smoking marijuana is still **against the law** and, because of new research that says **it is harmful**, it will never be made legal, (Bet on it), and B) you must realize that a kid who is a frequent marijuana user is now exposed to the shabby and classless world of **immediate gratification**. Anyone who is using drugs to cope with life is in **trouble**. This means good-bye to mid and long-range goals, good-bye career and great achievements, good-bye to the power to help others, and good-bye to feeling good about yourself. With drugs, the only way to feel good is to get "high." Emotional growth is stopped cold by drugs.

Of course, those who enter the sordid world of unearned highs say good-bye to friendships with winners and hello to friendships with losers, who as takers, cheaters, and thieves, have no self-discipline. The social lines in junior and senior high school between "druggers" and "non-druggers" are uncrossable. These lines are much more definitive than monied or unmonied, athletes or non-athletes, "goody-goody" or "cool" students. Kids who take drugs **always** hang-out with other kids who take drugs.

I don't mean this to sound like "Reefer Madness," that hilarious film of the thirties which told of death and destruction for those who smoked marijuana. Certainly as some of you read, your thoughts are on those "high-ranking professionals" of your acqaintance who regularly use marijuana and do not believe what I am saying here. If this is your refutation of my argument, keep this in mind: Kids are not "high-ranking professionals" possessed of enormous drive and a sense of self-determination, self-discipline, and, self-esteem. Of course, those "high-ranking professionals" will pay a price for their habit when their children find their "stash."

Parents and teachers know that lighting the fires of creativity and energy for academic endeavor is sometimes difficult to do for students who **have** a measure of energy for self-development. Sitting by quietly when we discover the cigarette papers, "bong" pipes, tin foil, "roach" clips, and other tools of drug use in his/her closet is not smart. This is **the** time to take action. Here are some steps we must take to **prevent** drug use among kids. After we discuss these steps, we will discuss other steps to take if we discover they are using already.

ONE   Pursue a vigorous drug education program in your family and your classroom. Do not assume the kids "know all about" hashish, marijuana, PCP, barbiturates, amphetamines, cocaine, and the rest. Make it your business to find out what these things do to the body, what they look like, how the kids get them, and what to do if you discover your child "high" on them. Make it your business to get **information** about substance abuse from your local school district, child conselors, social workers, psychologists, psychiatrists, drug "hotline," family counseling centers, and the library, so if your teens or pre-teens ever say "It's no big deal," you have the facts in addition to your fears.

TWO   Openly discuss in front of your children **your** friends who have made poor choices about illegal drugs **and** alcohol. Include your children in these discussions and solicit their opinions early as to what went wrong and why.

You will learn much about how your children feel about substance abusers, so listen! Communication means they have an opportunity to speak also.

THREE   Avoid arguments about substance abuse. If your posture is dig in and fight to the death, you may force your kids to defend a position they take out of a sense of fairness rather than solid belief. Remember, after a **discussion** everyone feels good because he/she learned and had an opportunity to share and give. After an **argument**, everyone feels bad because negative messages were exchanged in futile efforts to change someone's mind. Discussions make winners; arguments make losers. If you want to argue, bring up politics, religion, relatives, or money, **but not drugs.**

FOUR   Raise and teach your children using a **Positive Discipline Plan**. Such a plan includes the rules for the behavior of the kids, the unhappy consequences **they** choose by breaking the rules, and the happy consequences which occur because they followed the rules. Such a plan (which I outline and discuss in **BOOK ONE**: *BUILDING POSITIVE SELF-CONCEPT IN KIDS*, J. Zink, 1981), **insures** that the kids understand your rules on drugs, alcohol, sexual behavior, school work, etc. Furthermore, such a plan demands that you develop consequences which are fair and workable **before** the trouble starts. This way you make the consequences in a quiet reflective moment and not in the middle of the panic in Needle Park. Finally, the absolute foolproof method for preventing drug abuse of any kind, is to make **lavish** and **precise** use of positive messages, sent when you **catch** them doing something **right**. This easy-to-say. sometimes difficult-to-do behavior on the part of parents and teachers builds into youngsters a sense of their own importance to the world and gives them positive self-esteem. Kids who feel very good about themselves and have a life mission or sense of purpose **do not abuse themselves** with alcohol or drugs. Nothing I know gives that sense of confidence and well-being to kids faster than the very important people in their lives saying something like this, "When things really get rough, I like having you around because, of all the people I know, I am certain I can count on you. When I ask you to do something, and you say 'You got it,' I love it. Joe, you are the finest son a man could ask for."

FIVE   Teach your kids **how** to turn down offers for drugs. Role play the scene. You know how it happens. Someone says, "Wanna smoke a joint?" Then teach them **exactly** what to say. I teach the kids how to look their associates in the eyes and say, with a firm voice, "No. It is not my style."

SIX   If **you** use drugs, you can expect your kids to try them. You had better talk about why and how you use them, since you are **the** role model. Don't try to hide it or fool them; **they can't be fooled**. If you have been smoking dope with your friends and your kids come home unexpectedly, don't tell them you've been cleaning the oven when they ask about the funny smell.

You might consider **not** using drugs while the kids are living in your home. As the good book says, "As ye sow, so shall ye reap." Keep it in mind.

SEVEN   Always share **before** there is any trouble what you will do if there ever is any trouble with drugs. Tell them **right now** that if you learn they are experimenting with or are in possession of illegal substances you **will** do some or all of the following (the choice is yours, of course):

1)   Call the police.

2)   Daily search their room, closet, and possessions.

3)   Refuse them car privileges.

4)   Discontinue their car insurance.

5)   Closely scrutinize their friends and develop a blacklist of undersirables and let them know in person if they are on it.

6)   Confiscate all "headshop" equipment.

7)   Confiscate the stereo, and, take their record collection.

8)   Lock up the electric guitar, electric piano, or drum set in your car.

9)   Insist on weekly therapy.

10)   Send them to live with their father in Grand Forks, North Dakota.

11)   Contact the parents of all their friends and tell everything you know.

12)   Start a parent support group for the purpose of monitoring the kids activites **all the time**.

13) Revoke all party attendance unless a member of the parent support group is **in attendance** at the parties.

14) Insist on weekly attendance at church.

15) Commit them for a 72 hour observation at the local dry-out hospital or clinic for kids on drugs.

16) Buy their clothes from unglamorous large discount houses.

17) Discover which parents supplied the drugs and prosecute them to the fullest extent of the law in criminal **and** civil court. (It is a felony in most states to supply minors—knowingly or unknowingly— with controlled substances.)

Remember this: Kids seldom **leave** their own community to get drugs. The sad truth is that in all communities in America (and other countries, too) they can find whatever they want right in their own backyard.

Now that we've discussed some steps you can take to prevent your kids from using illegal substances, let's talk about what you can do if you discover they are using now.

ONE Don't freak out. Of course you are upset, angry, and feel betrayed. This discovery, more than almost (homosexuality comes to mind here) any other discovery about your children will put great emotional distance between you and them. This comes at a time when **both of you need each other most**. Step one is to do nothing until you calm down to the point where you can discuss the problem **with another person** without getting emotional or angry. Until that point, you are not prepared to discuss this with your son or daughter. If you are not prepared for this discussion, you will accomplish nothing by having it. Call your minister, priest, friendly local professional counselor, mother, father, close friend and talk out your feelings and **ask for their support**. You will be surprised how much love is out there and how many people love you! Do not be embarrassed to share your burden with others; you will discover the size of their burdens, too. Go to someone you can feel comfortable hugging and ask them for an old-fashioned hug. It does wonders!

TWO   If another parent had the courage to call you and tell you that your kid is using, call that wonderful person back and thank him or her and get more information now that you are calm.

Many parents do not call and tell other parents what they saw or heard because they do not want to carry tales—or, as the kids say today "Narc on somebody." ("Narc" has become what "fink," "squeal" or "rat" was to previous generations.) Don't be silly. Call them and tell them. Maybe they will have to do the same thing for you. And wouldn't you want to know?

THREE   Construct a plan of action **before** you interview your son or daughter. Decide your possible responses if you discover the problem is serious, mild, or an obvious experimental first of-fense. If you suspect the problem may be grave, talk to an entrance counselor at the local drug dry-out clinic (see the yellow pages) or hospital. Be prepared, if the problem is serious, to put the kid in the car and take him or her to the hospital or clinic immediately.

One other thing: Call the police and have a talk with the detective in charge of juvenile narcotics. Find out their policies on the various narcotics offenses including **pro-secuting** adults (also other parents!) who knowingly, or **unknowingly**, supply the kids with illegal substances. In most states, it is a **felony** to supply minors with even an ounce of marijuana. Not to mention other illegal substances.

Now that you are feeling prepared, supported, loved, grateful, encouraged, and have some legal knowledge of the problem, you are ready to talk to your kid.

FOUR   Pick your time and place to talk; limit the participants. Father, mother, and offender (rough word, huh?) is a good start. Getting other members of the family involved is essential, but not at this point. Make sure you will not be constantly interrupted by phones, television, visitors, etc. **This is important** so treat it with all the dignity of a critical corporate board meeting because there **is** a crisis at hand. If you do not handle the stockholders well, your company could go down in flames. Have an agenda. Keep it simple. It does not need to be written down, but it could read like this:

1)   What you were told or discovered. Stick to the facts and don't argue. Don't get emotional.

2)   Time for him/her to respond (please listen and do not interrupt!).

3)   Statement of your position on substance abuse in the future, including **all** possible consequences:

            A) Loss of TV, stereo, telephone, privileges, etc.

B)   Loss of the use of the car.

C)   Your revoking of his/her driver's license.

D)   Temporary institutionalization in hospital or dry-out clinic, etc.

E)   Full time drug therapy program—group and individual meetings for at least a year.

4)   A contract between you and the kid stating what **you** will do if he/she discontinues use in the future, like:

A)   Spend more time together.

B)   Share more activities together.

C)   Material goods which may be earned by staying "straight," etc.

5)   A **positive** conclusion to the meeting with a restatement of **everyone's responsibilities** to conquor the problem. Hugs and touching are in and ok. Tears are out.

A final word on substance abuse. If your son or daughter or your students choose a way of life which includes substance abuse, stop feeling guilty. You have your own life to live and you will not do a decent job of living it if you are riddled with guilty feelings. Life, after all, is a never ending series of choices and we all got where we are by making good or bad ones. Choosing to feel guilty about someone else's bad choice is a bad choice in itself. It robs you of the **confidence** you need to help those who need your help to learn to make **good choices**.

NOTES

Chapter Eleven:

SEX AND KIDS

Any discussion of sexual behavior and children must first focus on home life and begin by acknowledging the obvious. The kids learn what is ok and what is not ok **from their parents**. Like it or not, parents, you are the sexual role models for your children. If they determine from your behavior that a certain amount of promiscuity is ok, then they will tend to emulate what **your** behavior has told them is acceptable. So the messages they get from home largely will dictate the amount of control they will exercise over their bodies.

In the second place, and very early I might add, they will gather information available from their friends. Some of this information may be accurate; most of it is **not** accurate. And they most assuredly will get from their friends the message that it is ok to experiment. Their friends will regale them with wild and often exaggerated stories. The general implication is that wonderful, mysterious, and very exciting things are happening at certain parties and your children are missing all the fun. The fear of being left out, ignored, passed by, and not involved is great among young people. This fear is intensified by the electronic and film media in particular which **all but screams** to our kids, "If it feels good, do it!" and, as so sage a Jewish mother-wit as Ann Landers says, "Once they have done it, they ain't gonna stop." The woman is right.

Once again sex is an area where parents, far more than teachers, must show leadership. This is true because teachers are often handcuffed by the more outspoken parents on the issue of what schools can and can not teach. In some states the situation on "family-life" components in the school curriculum is handled with as much legislative care as is religion. Here are some common-sense approaches to handling sexual interests and preparing your children for sexual experiences so when the time comes, they can be comfortable with their bodies and make the right choices.

ONE   Give them the information early. Tell them **more** than they want to know rather than **less**. You will not hurt them, warp their minds, turn them into homosexuals, or any of the other popular tales relating to being **informationally** explicit with children. Your willingness to discuss sexual matters with them indicates your openness on the subject and when something does worry or scare them, they will bring it to you. One other point. You will know when what you are telling them is **more** than they can process because their facial expressions will go as blank as if you started to speak Russian to them. When this happens, wrap up the discussion with, "Thanks for asking me. I'm glad to share these things with you because it makes me feel like a responsible father (or mother)."

TWO   Give them guidelines for their sexual behavior. If running around the house naked is **out**, tell them, and enforce it. If sexual teasing annoys you, make a rule and stick to it. If masturbation bothers you, tell them no and mean it. If you are against open mouth kissing during dates and "exploratory touching," say it. Above all, if you are embarrassed by discussing the subject, **tell** them that; they will understand. Believe me kids are the most understanding and tolerant creatures on God's green earth. But, for their own sake, get past your embarrassment and give them **answers** to questions like, "How far is it ok to go?"

If you do not give them extremely explicit guidelines for sexual behavior, **you** must share the guilt and pain when they made a bad decision. But, if you told them all they reasonably need to know and you have given them good guidelines, then, at least, you need not feel guilty when they make a bad choice. The pain you have always with you, of course.

One final point. If you can't possibly discuss sex with them, and it is clear by their questions, it is **the** time, then pay someone else to tell them. Your friendly local therapist will be happy to spend an hour with your son or daughter and discuss everything from aspirin to vibrators. I do this for parents all the time, but if you want my candid opinion, the job belongs to you.

THREE   What ever you tell them, always emphasize that sex is **heavy responsibility**. One gifted family-life teacher I know makes her students carry a five-pound bag of flour around for nine weeks. The high school students must not let any harm come to their little charges. One mother, picking up the spirit of the experiment, set her daughter's alarm for 2 am and taped a note to it which read "Albert is hungry." Of course, the subject of responsibility can get heavier. Your discussion should include, in descriptive languages, what happens **during** an abortion as well as what happens after. The thought of terminating a pregnancy often weighs heaviest on a young mother **years** after the abortion. After all, during an abortion, a little part of you does die. These things **must** be told to youngsters.

Not long ago, a 15 year-old was in my office and told me she felt certain she would not get pregnant because after she had intercourse with her boyfriend**s**, she "jumped up and down. It confuses the sperm," she told me. When I told her that there are up to 400 million little squiggly things all fighting for the chance to "score," and that they will hide up to three days inside her body waiting for the right moment, she said something that **you** should never forget, "Why didn't someone tell me this?" An excellent question. **DO NOT THINK** because "They know so much more than we did at their age," that they are adequately prepared with scientific knowledge. As an educator who deals daily with "sophisticated and worldly

Southern California kids," I will tell you point blank: They **rarely** (one out of one hundred) know what they **need to know** in order to make intelligent decisions about sex.

FOUR — Do not treat sex as a taboo subject in your home. Face it, folks. Queen Victoria is dead. Since 1901. I recommend when the subject comes up a little light-hearted humor goes a long way toward demystifying the reason we all get our start in life. Sex is very much a part of the human condition. To deny it by saying "We don't talk about such things around here" is to invite neurosis. Stop being so threatened by sex. It won't bite you, and if it does, it might feel good. And that is a big wink from Dr. Zink.

FIVE — Speaking of winks, keep a close eye on your children's friends. It is your inalienable right as a parent to screen your children's friends. Don't let them hang around with creeps. But make sure they **are** creeps before you put them on the list of undesirables. This involves spending time socially with your children's friends. A list of suggestions for helping children choose good friends may be found in Chapter Five.

SIX — Once it has been determined that your

children are having sexual intercourse, it is fairly unreasonable to expect them to abstain. At this point you must make sure they understand all about preventing pregnancy (assuming they wish to prevent it), venereal disease, and the dangers of cervical cancer from multiple sex partners. No discussion of sexual intercourse is complete without coverage of herpes simplex II. This insidious virus can make a social leper out of the most popular teenager in a few minutes flat. The presence of the herpes simplex II virus has dealt a major blow to the fast and responsibility-free life of the singles scene. The word is slowly filtering through the high schools and (yep!) junior high schools. Like recent Supreme Court decisions, a renewed effort by concerned citizenry to reinstate the dealth penalty, use-a-gun, go-to-jail laws, and other indications that the age of permissiveness is over, indiscriminate sexual intercourse has been found to carry a very high emotional price. Most teenagers are simply unprepared to pay that price. Our job, as parents in particular, is to state in unequivocal, but emotion-free terms exactly what constitutes the price and how they will have to pay.

SEVEN   Even when your youngsters choose to ignore your advice and recommendations on sexual matters, keep on communicating. Your willingness to talk indicates the extent of your love. Withholding communication because you disagree with their sexual behavior will not help them learn to make good choices. You can be an effective communicator **and** totally disagree with their lifestyle. Throwing them out, slamming down the phone, dissolving into tears and other demonstrations only fails them at a time when they **need you the most**. Anybody can be a champion parent when the kids are well-behaved; it takes a star to face the tough issues with courage, calm, and, as John Denver says, "The serenity of a clear blue mountain lake."

EIGHT   Remember, it is a basic immutable law of the universe that each generation has the right to discover its own ways of coping with the eternal problems of life. Ecclesiastes is right. "One generation passeth away and another cometh; the sun also rises." Try and keep a more global perspective when dealing with sexual development of your children. Remember how much we thought we knew when we were

young and remember how very, very
little we actually did.

NINE   There is nothing stopping you from
teaching them that sex is among the
finer ways to say, "I love you." It is,
after all, the ultimate positive message
when one human offers
himself/herself totally and without
reservation in an act of giving and
sharing.

Romance need not be lost even to the generation that
can never be surprised because of what it saw on cable
television.

Stress to your children the importance of holding,
touching, and love's own special embrace. Teach them
love is a gift you can never completely give away because
it always comes back in more wonderful ways than you
gave it.

Finally, show them in little, simple ways how you care
for your own life mate. John Lennon was right, "And in
the end, the love you take is equal to the love you make."

Chapter Twelve:

IN SUMMARY

And Jesus rebuked him; and the devil went out of him; and from that moment the boy was cured.

Then the disciples came to Jesus privately and said, "Why could not we cast it out?" He said to them, "Because of your little faith; for then I say to you, if you have faith like a mustard seed, you will say to this mountain, remove from here; and it will remove. And nothing will be impossible to you."

St. Mathew
Chapter 18
Verses 17-19

In the pages of this book I have written words which symbolize ideas about motivating children. These words are only so many black marks on a white page. They will remain in this useless state until you make the choice to use these ideas and make them work for you.

Kids who are not doing what you want them to do are not bad, evil, or necessarily lazy. There are no good kids. There are no bad kids. There are just kids. Sometimes they make good choices; sometimes they don't. They make bad choices because they see no good reason to make good choices. You can teach them that success is the best reason to make good choices.

If you choose to use the principles this book teaches, and if you believe in yourself sufficiently to adapt these principles to meet your own needs, then nothing can stop you from structuring successful experiences for young people. But you must give young people a good reason to work hard. Whether it is to please you, please themselves, or test themselves, good work happens for good reasons. And when they have done good work, they will feel it. When they get hooked on **that** feeling, the battle to get them to work is over.

The story of Miguel is appropriate here. Miguel was a sixth grader who did no work in school at all. Not a behavior problem, he sat and stared out the window, talked to his friends, look suitably ashamed when his teachers scolded him, but **he did no work**. His parents had failed to teach him how to work at home. They made his bed, his food, cleaned his dishes and his bathroom, bought his clothes, shined his shoes, supplied him with soap, toothpaste, toothbrush, and even ran the sweeper in his room. They did all these things for him, because they thought **all good parents do these things for their children**.

When Miguel waltzed home with five F's on his first report card in junior high school, they were in shock. How could Miguel do this to us when we are such good parents, they thought. It never occured to them that by doing everything for Miguel, they not only removed good reasons for him to work for himself, they failed to teach him how to work. So Miguel, at age 12, did not know how to get things done. No wonder he felt so bad about himself.

Kids like Miguel are what I call pleasure machines. They search for what entertains them, makes them feel good in a hurry, and helps them escape from the pain of those around them insisting that they **do** something to con-tribute to the general welfare and pay for some small part of their "cost" of being alive.

If Miguel does not learn to earn part of his keep now, he probably never will. Or his growth toward an ultimate goal of self-reliance could get permanently stunted by his search for "the easy way" to obtain successful feelings about himself.

There has been always an "easy way" to those good feelings. For most young people today, it is drugs. Drugs provide what some drug and alcohol counselors call an "unearned high." "Earned highs" may be distinguished from "unearned highs" in this way:

To get Miguel working, I trained his parents to praise him when he did something on his own and to **stop doing everything for him**. Simple verbal and non-verbal praise (smiles, pats, thumbs-up, etc.) were powerful positive messages for Miguel. When he made his bed and his parents expressed their happiness, Miguel "earned" the high he received from their praise of his work. Furthermore, I trained Miguel's teachers to award Miguel's work in class by signing a card which he carried to each class. Each teacher's signature was worth ten minutes free time in the computer room after school. I did this because Miguel told me he was fascinated with computers and someday he would like to be a programmer. Always ask kids about their career plans because it is a wonderful way to discover what they think will help them feel good about themselves or, in the parlance of the street, get "high."

So when Miguel received ten minutes of computer time for working in class, he "earned" a "high."

Now the rub. Kids today want to skip the work and get to the "high." These are called "unearned highs" and Miguel is, at age 12, a classic candidate for drugs, alcohol, stealing, subversion, law-breaking, irresponsible sexual behavior, and all the other common pursuits of **undisciplined** teenagers. We can say this with certainty even though he is still one innocent little boy who hasn't learned how to work because his parents never taught him. Looked at another way, by being "good" parents and doing everything for him, and buying him everything money can buy, they unwittingly cheated and robbed him of learning how to "earn" his own "highs." For Miguel, driven to seek highs as are all of us, the short cut is the unearned high unless our work with him teaches him something before some other kid hands Miguel his first joint. In Miguel's case I am pleased to report some early positive results but the next twenty-four to thirty-six months will tell a lot about his chances for solid success at being a self-disciplined person. It is a race with precious time. I hope we all win.

In a larger sense, we are all in a race with time when we raise and teach children. Now, more than ever, it is clear that the future of our planet and potential lives of the unborn depend on our ability to teach our children self-discipline. If we are to find solutions to the giant problems which face us in the remaining days of our lives, we must produce children who find happiness and fulfillment in confronting and solving those giant problems. We must be more successful at producing children who like to work. To work well, they will need energy, creativity, imagination, and, above all, the self-discipline to stay at the task. Which is a particularly fitting statement to end this task for me.

In writing this book I feel I have contributed to the common good. God has blessed me with strength, time, and good fortune to finish it. For me this is an "earned high" and I feel very good about myself because I have written this last sentence. Thank you for sharing this moment with me. Wherever you are now and wherever I am when you read these words, for a few brief hours our lives connected in a common bond of love for kids. Don't waste the energy we both brought to the task. Thank you, God bless you, and (once more with good solid emotion!),

GO GET 'EM!

NOTES

TEACHERS: Use this chart as a model for your classroom. Fill it in, print it on large poster board. Post it **in front** of your classroom, and **use it every day**.

THE ZINK METHOD

CLASS RULES

1. _____

2. _____

3. _____

4. _____

5. _____

REWARDS (What happens when you follow the rules!)

1. _____

2. _____

3. _____

NEGATIVE CONSEQUENCES (What you choose by breaking one or more of the rules.)

1. A verbal warning

2. Loss of a privilege for a short time

3. _____

Remember: Negative consequences do not promote good behavior; they stop bad behavior. Positive consequences promote good behavior. So catch them being good!

GO GET' EM!

PARENTS: Cut out, fill in duplicate, and post at least three places:
1) The refrigerator   2) The bathroom, and 3) The kids' rooms.

THE ZINK METHOD

HOUSE RULES

1. _____

2. _____

3. _____

4. _____

5. _____

REWARDS (What happens when you follow the rules!)

1. _____

2. _____

3. _____

NEGATIVE CONSEQUENCES (What you choose by breaking one or more of the rules.)

1. A verbal warning

2. Loss of a privilege for a short time

3. _____

Remember: Negative consequences do not promote good behavior; they stop bad behavior. Positive consequences promote good behavior. So catch them being good!

You are the most important person in you child's life, so put some passion and enthusiasm into your praise!

GO GET' EM!

THE CHAMPIONS SERIES
by
Dr. J. Zink

BOOK ONE: $9.95

Praised by teachers and parents as the most straight-forward and easy to read approach to positive discipline, **Building Positive Self-Concept in Kids** will give you hundreds of good ideas for making your relationship with kids a positive experience. This book will train you to build a step-by-step positive discipline plan.

BOOK TWO: $9.95

Motivation problems? Discipline problems? Drug, Alcohol & Teen Sex problems? This book will give you answers! Written in an easy-to-understand style, **Motivating Kids** will give you novel and effective solutions to the bewildering array of troubles that parents and teachers face today.

BOOK THREE: $9.95

EGO STATES is the culmination of the champions trilogy. Here Dr. Zink explains why we lose our tempers, harbor anger, and engage in self-destructive behaviors which further erode our self-esteem. Here are the EXACT steps to take to become more loving and feel more competent as parents and teachers. Whatever you do, don't miss this one!

DEARLY BELOVED: SECRETS OF SUCCESSFUL MARRIAGE $19.95-(Hardbound Only)

Working on the theme of three parts in marriage (sex, intimacy, and commitment) and drawing on his experience in private practice, Dr. Zink departs from his usual subject of child behavior to focus on marriage. Written to celebrate their 21st wedding anniversary, **Dearly Beloved** includes commentory by Dr. Zink's wife, Kern. Here are their secrets of their successful marriage spelled out in plain talk. Don't be married without it!

THE AUDIO TAPE: $14.95

Hear Dr. Zink explain how certain messages destroy and certain messages build a positive self-concept in children and young adults. A motivating and emotional experience, this one hour tape will get you charged up and on a positive track for getting kids to behave. This tape will teach you to follow-through on a positive discipline plan for home or school.

Video Tape One For Parents: The Rules $34.95

Here Dr. Zink describes the very specifics that positive parents use to write the rules for the behavior of their children. This no-nonsense approach includes help for divorced and blended families. (VHS only)

Video Tape Two For Parents: The Prices $34.95

This tape teaches what positive parents do and say when the kids break the rules. Prices are not punishment, Dr. Zink shows clearly, and when you learn this special skill, you are on your way to being a positive parent. (VHS only)

Video Tape Three For Parents: The Positives $34.95

Catching our kids following the rules is what we all know we should do. Here Dr. Zink shares the secrets of the most positive parents as they develop a loving, positive, and powerfully fulfilling relationship with their children. It is never too late to begin! (VHS only)

Video Tape Four For Parents: The Zink Money System $34.95

Thousands of parents have been thrilled with the remarkable effectiveness of this system which replaces allowances for kids with an efficient method for teaching the value of money while building self-worth. (VHS only)

Video Tape Five For Teachers: Classroom Discipline $99.95

Here is the tape educators have been waiting for! Eighty minutes crammed with hundreds of useful ideas organized into a simple system for effective classroom discipline! No one can motivate teachers like Dr. J. Zink. (VHS only)

Video Tape Six For Teachers: The Most Asked Questions On Discipline. $99.95

In this live session, today's classroom teachers ask Dr. Zink many of the penetrating and very relevant questions facing educators concerned with discipline. Witty and poignant, some of Dr. Zink's answers may surprise even veterans. (VHS only)

THE COMPLETE CHAMPIONS WORKSHOP AUDIO TAPE: $49.95

And introducing for the first time ever, the complete Dr. J. Zink CHAMPIONS WORKSHOP on audio tape! **Three hours** of fun and fulfillment. On March 5th, 1986, Dr. Zink gave what many consider to be the finest workshop of his professional life to 500 educators in La Porte, Indiana. Here, for the first time, is the complete sound track to that workshop. Dr. Zink, in his own humorous style, teaches his ENTIRE POSITIVE DISCIPLINE PROGRAM on high quality audio cassettes. You will laugh, cry, and learn how to get YOUR needs met while raising and teaching kids!

THE ZINK BULLSEYE CHART: $9.95

Here is the famous Bullseye Chart that has proven so effective in raising academic and behavior performance in kids. 22X34 inches, this plastic-coated, **reusable** progress grade chart teaches kids how to track their own progress. It is ready to hang on the back of their bedroom doors and raise those grades!

THE GUIDES: $3.95 (each)

Champions on the School Bus and **Champions in the Library**. These guides for positive discipline were written specifically for school bus drivers and librarians. In very clear language, these unique pamphlets describe specific techniques to help kids feel good about themselves for behaving on the bus and in the library. No school bus and no library should be without one.

You will believe you can make champions.

Dr. Zink, please send:

_____	Copy(s) BOOK I (Self-Concept)	@	$ 9.95	= $ _____
_____	Copy(s) BOOK II (Motivation)	@	$ 9.95	= $ _____
_____	Copy(s) BOOK III (Ego States)	@	$ 9.95	= $ _____
_____	Copy(s) DEARLY BELOVED (Secrets of Successful Marriage)	@	$19.95	= $ _____
_____	Copy(s) CHAMPIONS AUDIO TAPE	@	$14.95	= $ _____
_____	Copy(s) CHAMPIONS VIDEO TAPES	@	$ _____	= $ _____
	Specify Tape Numbers _____			
_____	Copy(s) THE COMPLETE CHAMPIONS WORKSHOP AUDIO TAPE	@	$49.95	= $ _____
_____	Copy(s) SCHOOL BUS	@	$ 3.95	= $ _____
_____	Copy(s) LIBRARY	@	$ 3.95	= $ _____
_____	Copy(s) ZINK BULLSEYE CHART	@	$ 9.95	= $ _____

Total Cost of Material Ordered $ _____

Shipping & Handling (10% of total cost; $2.50 min.) $ _____

Shipping & Hanldling outside U.S.A. (10% of total cost; $5.00 min.) $ _____

CA Residents only: Add 6 ½ % of total cost $ _____

Total amount enclosed $ _____

ORDER MUST BE ACCOMPANIED BY PAYMENT IN FULL. SCHOC
DISTRICTS: PURCHASE ORDER IS OK.

Make check payable to:
> J. ZINK, INC.
> P.O. BOX 3279
> MANHATTAN BEACH, CA 90266

PLEASE SHIP MY MATERIALS TO: (PRINT)

_____

NAME

_____

STREET & ADDRESS

_____

CITY   STATE   ZIF

Note: For VIEDO TAPE VHS format only.